Earthquakes

and

Young Volcanoes

along the Eastern Sierra Nevada

at Mammoth Lakes 1980, Lone Pine 1872,
Inyo and Mono Craters

By C. Dean Rinehart and Ward C. Smith

Edited by Genny Smith

1982

Distributed by William Kaufmann, Inc.
95 First Street
Los Altos, California 94022

Scientific illustrator: Ann E. Kook

Photographers: Malcolm M. Clark, La Moine R. Fantozzi, W. D. Johnson, T. J. Johnston, Lester Lubetkin, Edwin C. Rockwell, John S. Shelton, David B. Slemmons, Roland von Huene, Robert E. Wallace, Robert Frampton.

Book Design: Linda Marcetti

Cover Design: Stephanie Furniss Design

Front cover: Mono Craters. Back cover: cinder cone and fault scarp south of Big Pine. Photos by Roland von Huene.

Copyright © 1982 by Genny Smith
Genny Smith Books, Palo Alto, California

ISBN 0-931378-02-8
Library of Congress Catalog Card Number: 81-51293

First printing February 1982

Contents

The Authors

Dean Rinehart, U.S. Geological Survey, mapped the geology of the Mammoth Lakes region during seven field seasons. He is co-author, with Donald C. Ross, of the geologic maps of the Mount Morrison and Casa Diablo quadrangles; and, with N. King Huber, of the Devils Postpile quadrangle. He and Huber co-authored "The Inyo Crater Lakes—A Blast in the Past" (*California Geology*, 9/65) and *Cenozoic Volcanic Rocks of the Devils Postpile Quadrangle* (Geol. Survey Prof. Paper 554-D, 1967).

Dr. Ward C. Smith, retired from the U.S. Geological Survey, is consulting professor in Applied Earth Sciences, Stanford University.

Genny Smith is the editor and co-author of the authoritative guidebooks *Mammoth Lakes Sierra* and *Deepest Valley: Guide to Owens Valley*. She and Ward live in their Mammoth Lakes cabin, at 9,000 feet, as much of each summer as they can manage.

Acknowledgments

Israel C. Russell in 1889 published the classic geologic work on the Mono Basin; and Adolph Knopf in 1915, the classic work on the Owens Valley. Following them have come dozens of earth scientists from many parts of the world, drawn by the extraordinary geologic features that here are so beautifully exposed. To all of them, who have built up our understanding of this region bit by bit, we express our gratitude and admiration.

We have drawn heavily on two works: *Volcanism, structure and geochronology of the Long Valley Caldera* by Roy A. Bailey, G. Brent Dalrymple and Marvin A. Lanphere; and *Mammoth Lakes California Earthquakes of May 1980*, edited by Roger W. Sherburne. The authors, however, take full responsibility for all interpretations made here.

November 1981   *C. Dean Rinehart*
                                                        Ward C. Smith

Cause of earthquakes: a modern drawing of an Ancient Hindu tradition

California Geology, January 1968

Terrified by earthquakes and exploding volcanoes,

we humans have long sought to explain such cataclysms. Ancient peoples often put the blame on angry gods or gigantic beasts.

Earthquakes emanated from the lurchings of a huge tortoise, according to the Ancient Hindus, for they and many Eastern people believed a giant tortoise balanced the earth on its back. Others believed in a monstrous elephant, while the Ancient Japanese pictured a giant carp holding up the world and shaking it with every flick of its tail.

We too, seeking to understand earthquakes and volcanoes and other natural phenomena, have concocted theories to explain them. If today's theories of earth movement are new to you—mountain ranges rising, valleys dropping, huge plates of the earth's crust sliding under and over each other —you may find them as bizarre as those of the Ancient Hindus. Earth scientists are just beginning to understand the marvelous workings of our planet, and   perhaps a hundred years from now many of today's theories will be replaced by others resting on new information. This small book focuses on what earth scientists have observed and how they explain the recent earthquakes and young volcanoes along a portion of the eastern front of the Sierra Nevada in California, between Owens Dry Lake and Mono Lake.

The Ring
of Fire

If you plot the world's 500 known active volcanoes on a map, you would find that a great many of them border the Pacific Ocean. If you plot the world's known earthquakes, you will find that most of them also border the Pacific. This great circle of volcanic and earthquake activity is called "The Ring of Fire." Earthquakes within the Ring of Fire have killed half a million people.

The Ring of Fire has long been recognized but only recently explained — by the theory of "plate tectonics." While you may find it hard to imagine that gigantic plates of the earth's crust drift slowly about on our globe, grinding past one another, this theory fits available information and is accepted by the scientific community today. The theory continues to be modified as new data are available, but in the simplest terms it proposes that the crust of our planet is divided into huge masses of rock called "plates." These rigid plates float upon a hot, viscous material that is many miles below the earth's surface. They move in various directions; and wherever they crunch together, all hell breaks loose as they grind and jerk against each other or thrust one under another. That's what is happening around the Pacific along the Ring of Fire. The continual movement, even though only at a rate measured in fractions of inches per year, releases tremendous energy and heat, accounts for many earthquakes and doubtless controls volcanic eruptions around the ocean margin.

All of California lies within the Ring of Fire. It has one active volcano—Mount Lassen, which erupted violently in 1915—and several areas where eruptions have occurred during the last few thousand years. It endures thousands of quivers each year, many too slight to feel, along numerous active faults. The most notorious is the San Andreas, partly because movement along it devastated San Francisco in 1906 and also because of its great length and evidence of huge offsets. Earthquake damage to property frequently runs into millions of dollars.

Lesser known, because its population is sparse, is the great 400-mile-long fault zone lying at the eastern base of the Sierra Nevada. Movement along this fault zone caused the magnitude 8.3 earthquake that demolished the small town of Lone Pine in 1872. Many small movements along this zone during 1978 and '79 culminated in four magnitude 6 earthquakes at Mammoth Lakes in

The Ring of Fire

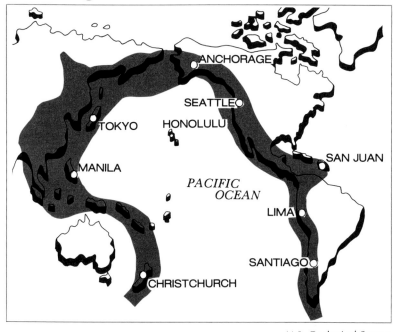

U.S. Geological Survey

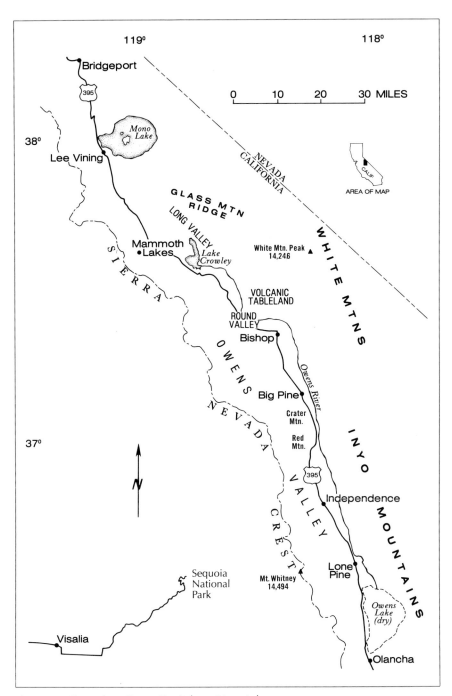

The Eastern Sierra, from Owens Dry Lake to Mono Lake

May 1980. A later sequence in September 1981 included two earthquakes greater than magnitude 5. Here and there, within this
unstable zone, molten magma has burst through weak places in
the earth's crust time and time again. At the Inyo and Mono
Craters, just south of Mono Lake, magma has erupted more than
twenty times during the last two thousand years.

Although the entire 400-mile-long Eastern Sierra Front has
shuddered repeatedly from faulting or volcanic explosions, we will
focus in the chapters that follow on the 130-mile portion lying
between Owens Dry Lake and Mono Lake. Here both historic
earthquakes and young volcanoes are abundant, and evidence of
their occurrence is unusually well preserved and easily accessible.
Most important, many geologists have studied this region in-
tensely. We pass on to you their understanding of this dramatic
landscape.

Mammoth Lakes Earthquakes of 1980

On Sunday morning May 25, 1980, the weather at Mammoth Lakes was sunny and a bit brisk, too. True, there were some clouds, but this was a day to stir enthusiasm for picnics, fishing the lower lakes, skiing the high slopes or watching the Hobie Cat races down at Crowley Lake. The bustle of preparing for the day was under way in many Mammoth households by 9:30. Three minutes later, minus a few seconds, activities slowed or stopped; many with keen senses knew immediately what was coming before it even started. It had happened so often during the past eight months they had almost, but not quite, gotten used to it. Faint vibrations — was it sound or had they felt it? — soon magnified and made the world a jarring, lurching, unstable thing, noisy now with the crash and tinkle of broken windows, fallen china, and smashed TV picture tubes. The uproar stimulated and at the same time paralyzed the urge to flee. Near the mountain front, the muffled thunder of rockfalls and avalanches prolonged the confusion of sound and motion and added the aerial spectacle of huge dust clouds rising as testimony of the mountains' protest against such rough handling. Three geysers, one 30 feet high, roared into action at Hot Creek, though none survived more than a few hours. Some new boiling pools appeared, while many existing hot springs and pools became hotter and more active. Even Lake Crowley joined in the action by disgorging great bubbles of gas in concert with the

jolting. Along the shore, a fisherman was thrown to the ground, and on McGee Creek another fisherman narrowly escaped thundering boulders that hurtled downslope after becoming dislodged by the quakes.

Thus it was that Mammoth Lakes reeled from the largest earthquake (M 6.1) in almost 40 years. During the next two days, the area was shaken by 300 tremors, three of which measured M 6.0, 6.1, and 6.2. The 600 earthquakes of M 3.0 or larger that jolted Mammoth between May 25 and August 1 proved to be the greatest earthquake activity along the entire Eastern Sierra Front during this century.

Seismograms of the Four Largest Earthquakes, May 1980

Time is Greenwich, 7 hours later than PDT. Recording stations are Berkeley, CA (BKS) and Jamestown, CA (JAS).

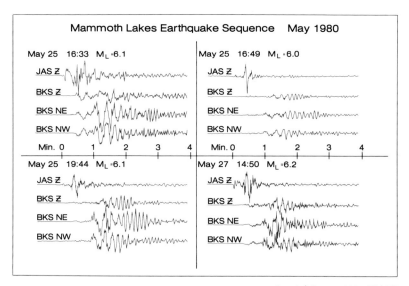

Special Report 150, CDMG

14

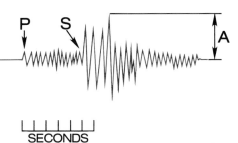

SECONDS

The Richter
Magnitude Scale

The Richter magnitude scale now in general use expresses the strength of an earthquake *at its epicenter* by a number, often with a decimal in it; we use M 5, M 6, M 6.3, etc. It is important to remember that between one whole number and the next the calculated strength increases or decreases 10-fold. Thus, M 6 is 10 times as violent as M 5, and M 8 is 1,000 times as violent as M 5. The scale does not have an upper limit. The lowest magnitude you can feel is about M 2, while the highest yet recorded is M 8.7.

Magnitude is calculated from dimensions measured on a recording made by a Wood-Anderson or other standard seismograph. By Richter's definition, a magnitude 3

earthquake will record a peak amplitude of 1 mm if the standard instrument is 100 km distant from the epicenter. For actual strength of the shake *at the instrument,* you measure the amplitude in millimeters of the maximum "wiggle" on the recording (A, above). The logarithm of that measured value is used, hence steps in the calculated magnitude scale change logarithmically. Strength decreases with distance from the epicenter, and to get this relationship into the calculation you take from the recording the time-lapse between arrival of the primary and secondary waves (P to S, above), which is proportional to distance.

Promptly following the first M 6.1 earthquake—swarming almost like aftershocks—came geologists, seismologists, and other geophysicists. Some brought seismographs, gravity meters, and other measuring devices; others brought cameras, maps, compasses, and notebooks. (John Muir's only instrument for his observations in Yosemite following the 1872 Owens Valley earthquake was a bucket of water kept on his table.) The scientists came from the universities of California and Nevada, from the California Division of Mines and Geology and U. S. Geological Survey and other government agencies, including the omnipresent Los Angeles Department of Water and Power. All the experts became sources of authoritative information in their special fields. After some initial confusion, a rapidly organized scientific clearing house based at the local fire station served the public and the news media.

Instrumental recordings and on-the-ground observation together have generated a mass of data that doubtless will give rise to many scientific treatises over the next few years. Because this area was known to be seismically active, several networks of recording instruments were in place already, strategically deployed to monitor local seismic events. Instrument sites included the Mammoth High School gym, a building along Convict Creek and an abutment of the Long Valley dam. After the initial quake, additional portable instruments were deployed for a time to monitor aftershocks.

Geologists combed the area recording all kinds of observations related to the earthquakes, acquiring information equally as valuable as recordings from instruments. They found and described earth ruptures, noting displacements, trends, continuity, and pattern; rockfalls and avalanches, their position and volume; landslides and soil disturbances of all kinds; changes in streams, cold and hot springs, and other geothermal phenomena; turbidity in lake waters; and damage to the works of man.

Overall estimates of damage by February, 1981, came close to $2,000,000. This included structural damage to buildings, roads, Whitmore Hot Springs, Hot Creek recreational area, the fish hatchery and contents of damaged buildings. Damage was diverse and widespread. The fish hatchery alone sustained damages of about $250,000. Extremely muddy water in the ponds hampered feeding operations and directly killed fish of all ages. Mortality would have been higher because of pile-ups at end screens, had not

16

Chimney Damage   Mono Herald

Earthquake Damage Mammoth Lakes, May 1980

Earthquakes began to jolt the Mammoth Lakes region with unusual frequency about September, 1979. The shaking culminated eight months later with four severe quakes M 6 or greater. No lives were lost and no structures collapsed, but damage to buildings, roads and ditches was diverse and widespread.

Mammoth Elementary School Library   Mono Herald

Epicenters and Area of Surface Rupture, Earthquakes May 25–31, 1980 Mammoth Lakes–Long Valley, California

Red dots indicate the epicenters of the May 25–31 earthquakes M 5 or greater; circled dots, the four M 6–M 6.2 quakes. Epicenters are sequentially numbered beginning with the first M 6.1 quake, May 25. Hypocenters— calculated depth below epicenter in miles to the "focus" or source of energy released—are shown in parentheses for the three deepest; hypocenters for the remainder lie at depths of 6 miles or less. Colored area marks zone of observed surface ruptures.

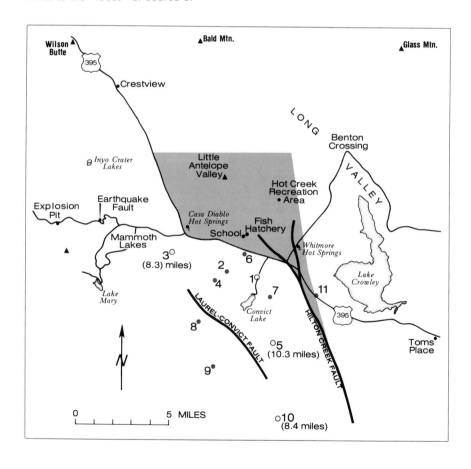

large numbers of trout been released into Hot Creek. For weeks thereafter, fishing in Hot Creek was unexcelled! Whitmore Hot Springs sustained another $250,000 in damage, although it was fully functional through most of the following summer. Many Mammoth homeowners faced broken water lines and accompanying damage by flooding, toppled or dangerously cracked chimneys, cracked walls and fallen plaster and dislocated beams. Total costs attributable to the earthquakes will inevitably increase, because more stringent building codes will be imposed for zones (to be designated by the State) within which recent movement along an earthquake fault can be demonstrated. For example, the entire Mammoth Elementary School will be relocated since it seems to sit astride an active fault.

New boiling pools, superheated fountains, and a general heating up of previously soothing, temperate waters forced temporary closure of Hot Creek. The Forest Service temporarily closed 150 square miles of the John Muir Wilderness in order to assess rockfall hazards. Some irrigation ditches were completely filled with soil that apparently liquified as a result of the shaking and flowed downslope into the aqueducts. No monetary value could be placed on the loss of home and mother by two baby porcupines, who wandered into Mammoth Village in search of help.

The map opposite shows the major earthquake activity of May 25–31, 1980. It indicates the epicenters of the largest temblors and also the area where most surface ruptures occurred. Confounding geophysicists and geologists alike, this map shows that only one epicenter is close to a mapped fault (Hilton Creek fault). Furthermore, that quake was one of the smaller events. Early reports quoted scientists as attributing the earthquakes to movements along the Hilton Creek fault. This is understandable because there hadn't been time to plot the epicenters accurately, and also because movement could reasonably be expected there. The remarkable 50-foot scarp in the following photographs is evidence of considerable recent movement along the Hilton Creek fault. However, most of the minor surface ruptures observed after May 25 along parts of the fault's trace can probably be accounted for by slumping of soft overburden along the old scarps.

19

Hilton Creek fault scarp, south of Convict Creek junction   Malcolm M. Clark

The Hilton Creek Fault Scarp

This striking 50-foot fault scarp, perhaps more than any other single feature, provides an all important clue to understanding the Eastern Sierra landscape. A clue to understanding why the Sierra front is so steep, and why lava flows and cinder cones and hot springs are common along the Sierra's eastern base.

Hilton Creek fault scarp, offsetting McGee Creek moraine fifty feet   John S. Shelton

Movement along the Hilton Creek fault, which created this scarp, is prehistoric, yet in geologic terms is so recent that erosion has scarcely affected the planar form of the scarp. This is especially remarkable when you consider that the scarp consists of loose bouldery gravel.

Though few are so well expressed as the Hilton Creek fault, hundreds of similar faults along the Sierra's 400-mile-long eastern front have undergone comparable movements over and over again as the range tilts higher. The earth forces that have left, as their signature, the lofty Sierra Nevada and the dramatic Hilton Creek Fault Scarp are the same forces that shook Mammoth yesterday and Lone Pine a century ago.

Surface Ruptures along the Hilton Creek Fault Trace

Movement on the Hilton Creek Fault was a prime suspect for the May 25 earthquakes, but the data proved it innocent after all. Surface ruptures along the old fault trace, exactly where one would expect them, were abundant. The displacements proved to be small, however—measured in inches. They probably do not reflect movement along the fault. More likely, they reflect slumping of the loose overburden (sand and gravel) along the old scarp.

Surface rupture,
McGee Creek Road

Mono Herald

Closeup, McGee Creek Road, showing displacement

Robert E. Wallace

Surface ruptures   Mono Herald

Surface ruptures   Mono Herald

Surface Ruptures East of Highway 395

The ground surface also ruptured in the 35-square-mile area shown on the map, p. 18. Most displacements were less than one inch. Maximum observed displacement was about one foot, but total cumulative displacement across a group of parallel cracks locally amounted to as much as a few feet. Much, but not all, of the small-scale displacement can be attributed to the slump of the unconsolidated material that blankets an irregular surface of harder material beneath the surface.

Surface rupture, Highway 395   Mono Herald

One M 5.0 epicenter (#11) is nearly coincident with the trace of the Hilton Creek fault, but no other epicenters of the May 25–31 sequence appear to be directly related to surface ruptures. Much of this region was snow-covered and inaccessible at the time of the earthquakes, and perhaps that is why no one saw surface ruptures there.

Most surface ruptures trended northwest and were in the 35-square-mile zone shown on the map. Though almost all ruptures were less than a quarter mile long, a few were more than three-quarters of a mile. The displacements along the cracks were typically either extensional (pull-apart) or normal (the material above a sloping fracture slipped downslope over the material beneath). Maximum observed displacement was about one foot, but total cumulative displacement across a group of parallel cracks locally amounted to as much as a few feet. Most displacements were less than an inch. Much, but not all, of the small-scale displacement can be attributed to the slump of unconsolidated material blanketing an irregular surface of harder material. Many of the ruptures are along previously mapped faults. Where they show vertical offset, it is usually down on the side away from the mountain, parallel to the previous displacement along the fault. A few examples of liquefaction were noted in the zone of surface ruptures. Seemingly firm but water-saturated sediment may become fluid when shaken and flow, often quite readily. Filling of irrigation ditches by liquified soil, cited above, is a striking example.

Minor cracking was reported along the trend of the "Earthquake Fault," about a mile and a half west of Mammoth Lakes. There, displacement was mainly pull-apart, like that of the large "fault" itself, but measured in millimeters rather than meters. It is reasonable to question whether or not this feature is indeed a "fault," since neither vertical nor horizontal offset has occurred. Nevertheless, it is precisely on the trend of a mapped fault, less than half a mile away, that shows vertical displacement of several feet. Unfortunately, the past tense must be used in describing these surface ruptures, for scarcely any could be found after only a few weeks, owing to frequent rains, animal activity and their fragile nature.

Enormous rockfalls and debris avalanches were perhaps the most spectacular events accompanying the earthquakes. The drama

24

Huge dust clouds rising from rockfalls, McGee Canyon, May 25, 1980   T. J. Johnston

Rockfalls and Rock Avalanches

Rocks of all sizes—delicately balanced on steep canyon walls for decades or perhaps centuries and then dislodged in seconds by the first big jolt—thundered downslope as huge rockfalls and rock avalanches. Subsequent shakes triggered more rockfalls and stirred up dust clouds that were visible many miles. The photo of dust clouds, above, was taken from the shore of Crowley Lake five miles away.

Rock and snow avalanches buried hiking trails under many feet of rock. Boulders weighing tons bounded downslope in great leaps, snapping off even large trees. Luckily no hikers were killed, although rockfalls in Yosemite Valley 40 miles away seriously injured two hikers.

Large boulder smashes corral, McGee Creek Pack Station   Special Report 150, CDMG

Rock avalanche buries Convict Creek trail up to 30 feet deep.   Malcolm M. Clark

Rockfall on top of snow,
McGee Creek Canyon

Malcolm M. Clark

Fifteen-inch pine tree, shattered by flying boulder

Malcolm M. Clark

of these colossal events is evident in the photographs, but such evidence is tame indeed when compared to a firsthand account by someone who was on the scene—especially someone as gifted as John Muir, describing a rockfall in Yosemite triggered by the M 8.3 Owens Valley earthquake of 1872:

> The sound was so tremendously deep and broad and earnest, the whole earth like a living creature seemed to have at last found a voice and to be calling her sister planets. In trying to tell something of the size of this awful sound it seems to me that if all the thunder of all the storms I have ever heard were condensed into one roar it would not equal this rock-roar at the birth of a mountain talus.
>
> The first severe shocks were soon over, and eager to examine the newborn talus I ran up the Valley in the moonlight and climbed upon it before the huge blocks, after their fiery flight, had come to complete rest. They were slowly settling into their places, chafing, grating against one another, groaning, and whispering; but no motion was visible except in a stream of small fragments pattering down the face of the cliff. A cloud of dust particles, lighted by the moon, floated out across the whole breadth of the Valley, forming a ceiling that lasted until after sunrise.
>
> John Muir, *The Yosemite*

Though a hundred times less powerful than the earthquake Muir experienced, the Mammoth Lakes earthquakes of 1980 also triggered rockfalls in Yosemite, 40 miles away, that seriously injured two hikers. No lives were lost at Mammoth, and slight injury to a single hiker in the Convict Lake area fortunately was the only one noted. This is indeed remarkable, for as many as 26 hikers were reported in the Convict Creek area at the time of the first M 6 quake.

On September 30, 1981, earthquakes once again severely shook the Mammoth region. The two largest measured M 5.9 and M 5.2. Mercifully the sequence was shorter lived than the 1980 sequence. The epicenter of the initial (M 5.9) shock plots precisely at the center of the Laurel-Convict fault shown on the map on page 18. Epicenters of the others generally overlap those of the May 1980 sequence.

28

Lone Pine Earthquake of 1872

The Lone Pine earthquake of 1872 may be the largest ever in California's recorded history. At the very least, it is one of our three "monster earthquakes," ranking with the two that centered at Tejon Pass in 1857 and at San Francisco in 1906. Determining the magnitude of the two nineteenth century earthquakes has been most difficult. No seismographs; no trained observers; the science of seismology (study of earthquakes) yet to be born; and until 1887, when Lick Observatory began sending out precise time signals, not even accurate time.

Even so, there is no doubt at all that the Lone Pine earthquake was monstrous and that it rates a magnitude of about 8.3. A rumbling and roaring around 2:25 a.m. awakened some that morning of April 6. But before they were fully awake, a few minutes later the earthquake struck with devastating force. It demolished the town of Lone Pine, cracked brick walls in Chico 300 miles away, triggered huge rockfalls in Yosemite Valley, shook most of the western states, and even rattled Salt Lake City far to the east.

Of Lone Pine's 250 or 300 people, 23 were killed and 50 were injured. Of Lone Pine's 59 buildings, 52 were totally or partly destroyed. *Every* adobe, brick, and stone building collapsed, including the two-story courthouse. Adobe brick laid without mortar of any kind was, unfortunately, the most popular building

29

Inyo County Courthouse, 1872   Photo courtesy Dorothy C. Cragen

Lone Pine Earthquake March 26, 1872

The Lone Pine earthquake may have been the strongest in all California history. At the very least, it is one of California's three monster earthquakes. The shock cracked brick walls 300 miles away and rattled most of the western states, as far east as Salt Lake City. A letter from John McCall of Lone Pine describes the terror. "My wife and little daughter, as well as myself, were buried in the ruins for an hour and a half; there were four feet of adobe upon us. We were living a mile and a half from anyone, and were nearly dead when taken out . . . . Everything lost."

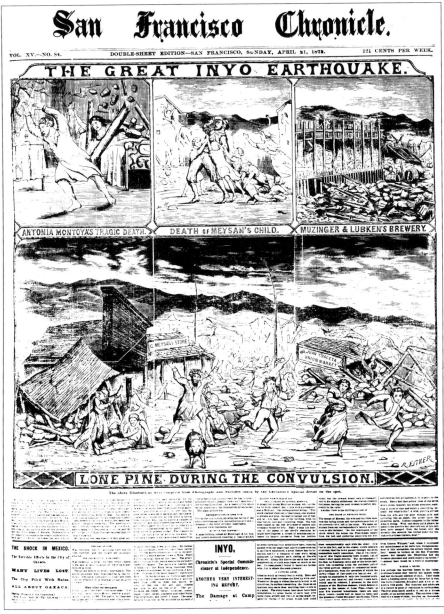

San Francisco Chronicle, April 21, 1872

The *San Francisco Chronicle* sent a correspondent to the scene, a six-day trip over Walker Pass. His account, with the illustration on this page was published a month after the event. The center drawing depicts the Meysan family's escape and their horror on discovering that one child was caught under the crumbling house. When the second story support walls of the brick courthouse gave way, the two floors pancaked.

material. It was plentiful and cheap, while lumber was scarce and expensive. Besides, adobe was a tradition with Lone Pine's many Mexican families who had come to work at the Cerro Gordo silver-lead mines. The adobe homes fell to pieces, walls and roofs crushing the sleeping occupants. Twenty miles away at Cerro Gordo, stone cabins collapsed and rock slides closed the road to the mines. Fifteen miles away at Camp Independence, several soldiers were killed by crumbling adobe.

Even brief notes on Owens Valley earthquake faults involve dimensions of fault displacements, and it seems desirable to note at the outset some dimensions of major elements of the landscape, as part of evaluating the region's earthquake history before the M 8.3 Lone Pine event of 1872. Faulting did play a large role in forming the landscape, for displacement on range-front fault zones raised, in a few million years, the Sierra Nevada on the west and the Inyo-White Mountains on the east, while the long block of bedrock between moved relatively downward. The structural trough, or basin, is Owens Valley. Of course, this is saying early that faults and accompanying earthquakes are not new here, that movements continue, and the outlook is for additional earthquake shocks in the forseeable future.

From Bishop and the Volcanic Tableland on the north, the valley trends about 15° east of south to Olancha at the southwest corner of the Owens Lake salt flat where Owens River ends. The distance along Highway 395 through the Owens Valley is 82 miles. The altitude change is from 4,002 feet to 3,648 feet, so small a drop that the Owens River course is conspicuously meandering on a nearly flat valley floor. The floor is mostly 2 to 5 miles wide, narrower where it passes the Big Pine volcanic field and the Poverty Hills, about 20 miles south of Bishop. Alluvial fans extend up to the base of the range fronts on either side, those in front of the Inyo-White Mountains smaller because the climate is much drier there. The Sierra fans are longest north of Lone Pine, the longest head at the range base a full 10 miles from the opposite Inyo fan heads. The fans effectively conceal most of the range-front faults on which the mountain blocks have been rising. The Sierra Nevada and Inyo-White Mountains crest lines are about 20 miles apart

Owens Valley: view northward from 15,500 feet, from near Lone Pine   John S. Shelton

Owens Valley

Meanders of the Owens River can be seen at the right edge, beyond the northern part of the Alabama Hills. Here the flat part of the valley floor is as much as 5 miles wide, and its elevations are below 3,900 feet. Recognizable in the distant center of the valley are dark cinder cones of Red Mountain and Crater Mountain. Just east of them, the river course runs close to the base of the Inyo-White Mountains, which rise abruptly in the east and culminate at snow-capped White Mountain Peak, elevation 14,246 feet. Long alluvial fans on the west side were built by strong streams of the Sierra Nevada. The deeply dissected Sierra scarp, mainly granite rock, rises to a crest with peaks above 14,000 feet. The highest is Mt. Whitney (just out of this picture to the left) at 14,494 feet.

at Mt. Whitney, but the valley opens much wider near Bishop because the pattern of range-front breaks changes greatly there. Peaks along the Sierra crest west of Lone Pine and the Alabama Hills include several above 14,000 feet, with Mt. Whitney at 14,494 feet; along the Inyo-White Mountain crest altitudes are mostly 9,000 to 11,000 feet, but White Mountain Peak is 14,246 feet.

Ruptures of the ground surface during the earthquake of 1872 raised fault scarps that have endured well, though perceptibly modified by weathering and erosion. The scarps mark the earthquake fault zone as being mostly north of Olancha and extending north to Big Pine. Some of the longer and higher scarps are near Lone Pine, displacing alluvial fans along the east face of the Alabama Hills.

Among the longer scarps are two south of Lone Pine: Diaz Lake is between them, being a sag pond on ground dropped between the faults. Note that the fault on the east extends through Lone Pine and beyond. At Diaz this scarp faces west, but beyond the cemetery north of town it faces east. The cemetery location is just west of Highway 395, on the uplifted side of the fault. The location is indicated by a highway sign. The fault continues north, parallel to the highway and quite near it, its course marked well by patches of vegetation because the fault acts as a barrier to underground water, which rises as seeps and springs.

It is not inappropriate to call the scarps we have been looking at, of even the whole Alabama Hills, "just the tip of the iceberg," because geophysical surveys across the flat floor of Owens Valley indicate that the valley fill east of the Alabama Hills is very thick. The depth to the bedrock underlying valley fill there is about 8,000 feet. The highest point in the Alabama Hills is at elevation 5,207 feet, roughly 1,500 feet above the valley surface, so you may visualize the east face of the hills as a scarp that rises about 9,500 feet above the buried bedrock floor. The Eastern Sierra front rising to Mt. Whitney is about that size, also. The point has been made that the bedrock surface below the fill is more than 4,000 below sea level, but must have been a part of the landscape above sea level at one time. Hence, it could not have stood still while the range blocks moved up along it; it must have been moved downward as part of the faulting.

34

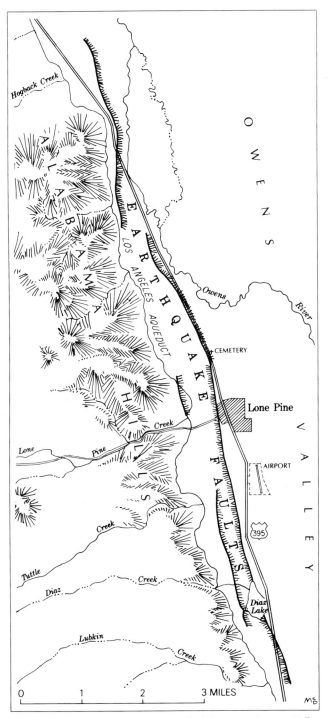

Paul Bateman, *Deepest Valley*

Map of Lone Pine, showing major fault scarps near east face of Alabama Hills

Hachures point to the down-thrown side and indicate which way the fault scarp faces. Diaz Lake is a sag pond on ground that subsided between two faults during the earthquake of 1872. Note that the longest scarp is west-facing through Lone Pine, and east-facing from the cemetary north. North of Lone Pine, scarps may be seen from your car window as you drive along Highway 395. Watch for east-facing banks of light-colored boulders, cobbles, and sand as much as 20 feet high. The cemetary of victims of the earthquake of 1872 is on the upthrown side of the long fault. About 4.5 miles north of Lone Pine, Highway 395 crosses an east-facing scarp, which is plainly marked by patches of greenery sustained by seeps along the fault.

Faults near Lone Pine

East-facing scarp, exposing boulders, cobbles and sands of upthrown alluvial fan. Height of this scarp ranges up to about 20 feet, but only a third of this is attributed to vertical displacement in the earthquake of 1872; the upper two-thirds shows effects of erosion following much earlier displacements.

Fault scarp west of Lone Pine

W. D. Johnson, USGS 1909

View northwest across Owens Valley toward Mount Whitney   U. S. Geological Survey

Shadowed scarps emphasize the fairly straight course of faults that separate the major structural blocks extending across this photograph: the Sierra Nevada block, with its peaks 8,000 feet above its range-front alluvial fans; the Alabama Hills with the highest point about 1,500 feet above the adjacent surface of down-dropped Owens Valley. Geophysical surveys across the valley here indicate that bedrock under the valley fill lies 6,000–8,000 feet below the surface. Without the valley fill, the east scarp of the Alabama Hills would rise as high as the main Sierra escarpment.

Evidence of successive uplifts: face of a young scarp   Lester Lubetkin 1978

Scarp about 20 feet high, raised by at least 3 uplifts. Debris pile along the base covers most of the youngest "face," exposed by uplift of 5 or 6 feet in 1872. The middle part, deeply washed, bouldery, and somewhat darkened by weathering, was exposed by earlier uplift. The uppermost part is much rounded back and quite darker from long weathering. The first uplift exposing this uppermost part may have occurred as long as 5,000 years ago. (Length of surveyor's rod is 4 meters, about 13 feet.)

Evidence of Repeated Uplifts

Weathering of the surface of this large boulder, which measures 10 by 15 feet as now exposed at a fault scarp west of Lone Pine, produced differences in roughness and darkness of bands which indicate successive uplifts. Only the freshest surface, below the geologist's hammer, was exposed by the displacement of 1872. The darker surface above, up to the darkest band, was exposed by uplift and consequent erosion following an earlier uplift. The very top of the boulder has a rounded and rough surface; it was the only part exposed above the original surface of the fan, and evidently the first uplift increased the exposed part down to the high dark band. The alluvial fan formed an estimated 10,000 to 20,000 years ago, so the boulder records at least two uplifts in that period, prior to 1872.

Evidence of successive uplifts: weathering of large boulder   Lester Lubetkin 1978

Looking north along Owens Valley toward mid-valley fault trace   John S. Shelton

Mid-valley Fault

The Manzanar air strip is in the lower
left corner, near the Los Angeles
aqueduct. Independence is the first
dark area north of it, near left edge.
In the photograph center, 3.1 miles
east of Independence, the straight
northwest-trending trace of a fault runs
for about 16 miles. It faces east, with
a scarp about 10 feet high near the
Citrus Road from Independence. A
concealed major fault at the base of
the Inyo Mountains on the east is
indicated by geophysical surveys.

Concealed Faults

A splendid photograph of Owens Valley features, large and small. The prominent white line along the Alabama Hills is not a fault scarp, it is the Los Angeles aqueduct. Note that it curves around a small alluvial fan near Lone Pine, at left edge of picture. The straight white line across this fan, west of the aqueduct, is an "earthquake fault of 1872." Its east-facing scarp is as much as 20 feet high. A much longer fault trace extends north from Lone Pine, parallel to the thin dark line of Highway 395 and just west of it. A dark patch of vegetation near the center foreground is on this fault trace. The Sierra range front shows, on a giant scale, triangular ridge ends between deep-cut canyons, characteristic features of an eroded fault scarp. These are present, less well-defined, on the Alabama Hills, also. Note that the major faults along the Sierra base and the Alabama Hills' east edge are quite concealed by alluvial fan and valley fill.

View westward of Eastern Sierra scarp, Alabama Hills and Owens Valley floor

John S. Shelton

At no time did the surface of the Alabama Hills, as we see it now, stand at the top of a great, fully exposed scarp some 8,000 feet high. If it ever held such a position, erosion during the time required for the Owens River to deposit the 8,000 feet of fill would have carved across the hills deep canyons like those we see on the Sierra Nevada escarpment. Such canyons would be identified today as embayments back-filled with Owens River sediment. On the contrary, we see valleys of moderate depth only, the streams that cut them having been limited in their down-cutting, obviously, to the present level of the Owens Valley floor. We also know that the granitic rocks of the western part of the Alabama Hills show evidence of having been buried, deeply weathered while buried, and exhumed. It seems probable that the Alabama Hills remained buried, all or most of the time, while the bedrock east of it subsided, probably step by step, for long enough (millions of years?) for Owens River to deposit the 8,000 feet of sediment there.

The Big Pine volcanic field includes basalt cinder cones and lava flows on either side of Highway 395 from just south of Big Pine to about 8 miles north of Independence. There are about 10 cones, some along the Sierra base, others close to the Inyo Mountains front; their lava flows extend down and partly cover alluvial fans. If you approach from the south, a conspicuous landmark off to the northwest is the cone of Red Mountain. From the north, Crater Mountain is the landmark because its summit cone is about 2,000 feet above the highway. Not all of its bulk is volcanic rock, however, because the granite of the ridge on which it is built shows through the lava cover in several places.

These basalts are reported to have ages of less than 100,000 years to as young as 10,000 years. Of first interest here are faults that displace flows as young as these.

The "best show on the road" can be found easily by leaving the highway 7½ miles sourth of Big Pine and driving west to the Poverty Hills. The view from the north slope of the Poverty Hills is along an eroded fault scarp nearly 80 feet high, which faces east. The fault displaced part of a small cinder cone as well as the fan on which it was built. Along most of the scarp the rounded condition

42

Faulted volcanic field: Crater Mountain and Red Mountain   John S. Shelton

Faults, Big Pine Volcanic Field

View southeast across the east flank of Crater Mountain's basalt lava flows. The conspicuous fault across the lava flows points to the Poverty Hills in the middle distance. Another fault (center, distance), which extends north from the west edge of the Poverty Hills, has significant features shown in the two photographs following. Red Mountain, the small cone in the distance on the right, is a cinder cone built upon the alluvial fan. Another fault, barely visible in this photograph, extends from Red Mountain to Crater Mountain.

Faulted volcanic field north of Poverty Hills   David B. Slemmons

Faulted volcanic field: cinder cone and fan north of Poverty Hills   Roland von Huene

Fault Scarp North of Poverty Hills

These low-altitude, oblique aerial photographs show details of the east-facing scarp that extends from the Poverty Hills north to Crater Mountain lava flows. Both views are northwest. The cinder cone and alluvial fan have been offset at least 80 feet vertically, but the large gullies cut into the scarp show that most of the movement occurred long ago. It probably involved more than one displacement. Note the longest gully above and left of the cone. As described in the text, the scarp crossing that gully is only 10 feet high. Probably this gully had its channel uplifted about 10 feet during the earthquake of 1872.

of the top, and particularly the presence of well-developed gullies show that the scarp is old, probably formed some thousands of years ago. Across a wash at its north end, however, the scarp is only 10 feet high. Here (photo p. 45), apparently, a small stream eroded and partly buried much of the old scarp. Then, probably during the 1872 earthquake, the gully channel was uplifted to about its present height.

You may continue west to another interesting fault by going south along the west edge of the Poverty Hills and turning toward the Sierra front on the well-traveled dirt road to a perlite quarry. Just east of the quarry the road crosses a west-facing scarp. The fault is a groundwater barrier, as shown by patches of vegetation and seeps. More interesting, perhaps, is that the fault extends from Red Mountain to Crater Mountain. Evidently it played a dual role here, its broken zone serving as a conduit for basalt, as well as being a fracture on which fault slippage occurred, rupturing the surface.

Back on the highway, one may see the north-trending fault which displaced lavas on the east slope of Crater Mountain. How much of the displacement occurred in 1872 has not been studied.

Other cinder cones in the Big Pine field are shown on geologic maps as situated on faults at the two range fronts. In spite of this evidence that the various conduits for the basalt were available, probably at various times over thousands of years, the total quantity of cinders and lavas extruded is small; one estimate is about 0.3 cubic mile.

Tomorrow's Earthquakes?

Round Valley, at the Eastern Sierra front 12 miles northwest of Bishop, is beyond the main Lone Pine zone shaken so severely April 6, 1872. Round Valley did receive, however, a strong aftershock estimated as M 6.9, which caused much destruction. Of interest now is the report that there has been a concentration of shocks M 5.5 or greater in recent years within a zone extending from Round Valley north to the margin of Long Valley. The seismic activity there has been greater than within any other segment along the entire 400-mile Eastern Sierra, leading to speculation

Epicenters of Small Earthquakes from January 1, 1970 to May 24, 1980 in Western Nevada and Eastern California

Red dots show epicenters of small earthquakes (M 2–M 5). Dense cluster of dots NW of Bishop is the 1978–1980 Mammoth Lakes sequence. Heavy black lines show faults; hachures show downthrown side. Recent movement along these faults (both historic and prehistoric) has rarely exceeded 20 feet.

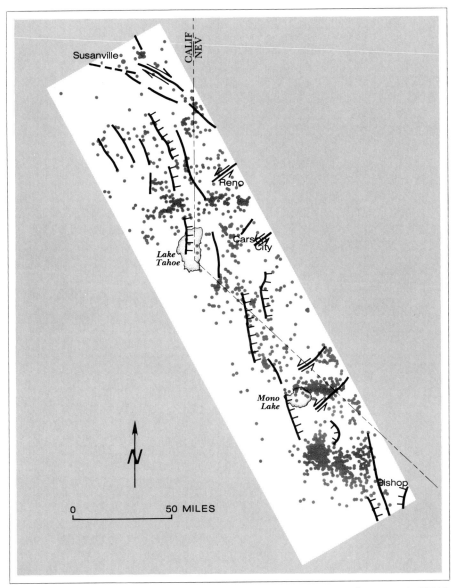

that this activity is precursory to a larger event. Seismologists Alan and Floriana Ryall of the University of Nevada, who have particularly studied patterns of seismic activity along the range front, concluded that this zone has the potential for an M 7.5 event. The May 1980 quakes at Mammoth, in the M 6 and M 6-plus range, came along later. Later still came M 5.9 and M 5.2 quakes early in the morning of September 30, 1981. But they were all less than one-tenth as strong as M 7.5, so we may consider the potential for much stronger shaking still remains.

The main Lone Pine zone has been remarkably quiet since the M 8.3 earthquake of 1872. Perhaps the zone offers opportunity for monitoring the condition of the fault blocks to identify some warning signals. A reliable method has not been developed yet — though a great deal of time, effort, and money is being spent to achieve the goal of precise earthquake prediction — in which the time, place, and magnitude of a quake will be anticipated within narrow limits. Progress is being made, and seismologists report promise, for example, in studies of how physical properties of rocks change under stress prior to actual breakage. Meanwhile, the 1872 ground ruptures and the great scarp of the Eastern Sierra tell us the ranges moved up in many steps, and more are sure to come.

And earthquakes are not all bad. A swarm of little ones underfoot may relieve Mother Earth's tensions and still move mountains, peacefully. Volcano observers pay considerable attention to all seismic events near their vicinity, seeking useful warnings of action under the ground that may precede an eruption. Such seismic warning signals could be invaluable in a populated area, depending greatly upon the type of eruption, if any, associated with the quakes. Along the main Lone Pine zone, there was no volcanic activity identified with the 1872 earthquake. At the Big Pine volcanic field, the young cinder cones and lava flows are closely tied to the surface ruptures or scarps. Again, the 1872 earthquake brought no new lava with it and, furthermore, the basaltic rocks there are typical of volcanoes of relatively quiet behavior when they do erupt.

The Mammoth Lakes-Mono Craters-Long Valley volcanic history included some eruptions of the quiet kind, but the main events were explosive. The dominant rock types are those com-

48

monly associated with violent eruptions. In that area, therefore, there may come a day when earthquakes give us a friendly warning and, if we can read it successfully, we might have time to move out to a safer spot. Whether it is Mammoth, or Round Valley, or Lone Pine, the next earthquake may take place while you are reading this sentence, or it may not come during your lifetime. Just one thing is certain: it will come.

Inyo and Mono Craters

One should not discuss earthquakes and movements along faults in eastern California without taking note of their intimate association with young volcanic rocks. Written history in this part of the world covers such a brief span that we must look elsewhere for historic records to document the association of earthquakes and volcanic activity. Today, news coverage of volcanic events is so complete that almost everyone knows that virtually all volcanic eruptions are preceded and accompanied by earthquakes. Almost everyone also knows that the vast majority of earthquakes are *not* accompanied by volcanic eruptions.

Here in Long Valley and the Mono Basin, however, where the recent geologic past is so generously populated with volcanic eruptions, the onset of earthquake activity raises legitimate concern that in this area the two phenomena may very well have a common derivation. This was certainly so at Mount St. Helens on May 18, 1980, just one week before the first M 6.1 temblor at Mammoth, for its mighty blast was apparently triggered by an M 5 earthquake. That, of course, raises the question asked most frequently after the onset of the Mammoth sequence: "Did the violent eruption of Mount St. Helens have anything to do with the earthquakes at Mammoth?" Most experts answered with an emphatic "no." Current understanding of the structural framework of the western United States indicates that volcanic activity in

Ages of Some Young Volcanic Rocks

Feature	Location on map	Approximate date of eruption*
Lava flow	#1 Negit Island	A.D. 1540 ± 300 yrs.
Dome	#2 northern Mono Craters	A.D. 1480 ± 200 yrs.
Explosion pit	#3 Mammoth Mountain	A.D. 1400 ± 150 yrs.
Explosion pit	#4 S. Inyo Crater Lake	A.D. 1400 ± 60 yrs.
Pumice and obsidian dome	#5 Panum Crater (N end Mono Craters)	A.D. 1240 ± 40 yrs.
Dome	#6 northern Mono Craters	A.D. 1000 ± ? yrs.
Domes	#7 & 8 Inyo Domes	A.D. 980 ± 250 yrs.
Obsidian flow	#9 near northwest end Mono Craters	A.D. 500 ± 300 yrs.
Obsidian flow	#10 NE margin Mono Craters	A.D. 75 ± 300 yrs.
Obsidian flow	#11 NE margin Mono Craters	B.C. 300 ± 400 yrs.
Obsidian dome	#12 Wilson Butte	B.C. 500 ± 400 yrs.
Obsidian dome	#13 S-central Mono Craters	B.C. 700 ± 800 yrs.

*Analytic uncertainty expressed by plus-or-minus values.

the Great Basin, whose western margin includes the volcanoes along the eastern front of the Sierra Nevada, is in no way related to volcanic activity in the Cascade Ranges of California, Oregon, and Washington, which include Mounts Lassen, Shasta, Hood, St. Helens, and Rainier. Hence, the close timing of the two events must be regarded as coincidence.

The potential for volcanic violence in the Long Valley-Mono Lake region has not escaped notice, however, for this region is one of three (the others, Mounts Shasta and Lassen) within California currently being studied under the U. S. Geological Survey's volcanic hazards program. These three were chosen partly because their volcanoes were active during the last two thousand years, but mainly because of their potential for explosive, catastrophic

52

Locations of Some Young Volcanic Rocks, Long Valley Caldera and the Bishop Tuff

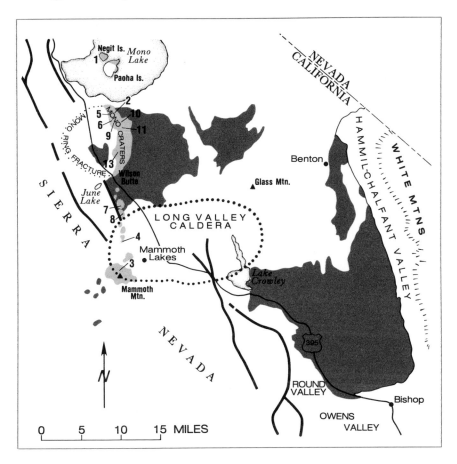

Map of the region between Bishop and Mono Lake, centered on the Long Valley caldera. Faults that define the eastern front of the Sierra, in heavy black. Bounding fault zone of the caldera in heavy black dots. Numbers refer to localities of dated samples; numbers and ages shown on accompanying table. Long Valley caldera is a huge depression from which the Bishop Tuff (red) blasted forth 700,000 years ago in a cataclysmic eruption about 200 times greater than the Mount St. Helens eruption of May 18, 1980. Bishop Tuff is the pinkish rock exposed in road cuts for many miles north of Bishop. As shown above, it covers about 450 square miles; drill cuttings and inclusions in younger volcanic rocks indicate a thick layer of Bishop Tuff also may underlie the entire caldera at depth. Mono ring fracture and the associated Mono Craters may represent early stages in the development of a future caldera.

eruptions. Local evidence shows that past eruptions here resemble those at Mount St. Helens: explosive eruptions involving the ejection of much medium- and fine-sized particulate matter accompanied by large amounts of vapor. A remarkable array of new rock-age determinations shows that in the Mammoth-Mono area alone, volcanic eruptions during the past 2,000 years have occurred at an average rate of one per century! All of these eruptions have occured along a linear zone 25 miles long, extending northward from Mammoth Mountain to Negit Island in Mono Lake. These eruptions include most of the volcanic domes of the Mono Craters as well as their southern extension, sometimes known as the Inyo domes, and the Inyo Crater Lakes. Although these eruptions were small compared with Mount St. Helens, pumice and ash from some have been identified as far as 60 miles away. Some of the youngest volcanic features and their approximate ages are shown on the accompanying table, map and photographs.

There is no reason to believe that this eruptive pattern will change in the foreseeable future. We may, however, take nervous comfort in knowing that at least nothing like Mount St. Helens has happened here in the last 2,000 years!

Lest we become too complacent, however, it is well to contemplate Long Valley—the site of the most colossal eruption in eastern California and western Nevada during the Ice Age, for which we have a geologic record. We now know Long Valley to be an inactive volcanic caldera—a fault-bounded elliptical basin (see map) whose floor sank to a depth of half a mile or more below sea level about 700,000 years ago. It sank when eruption emptied an underlying chamber of magma (molten rock). During this catastrophic episode the volcano erupted fine ash, pumice and an incandescent frothy mixture of the two that cooled and hardened to form Bishop Tuff, the familiar reddish, porous rock that blankets about 450 square miles of the surrounding area (see map). Besides overflowing Long Valley northward into Mono basin, good evidence exists that the Bishop Tuff also overflowed westward into the San Joaquin's Middle Fork Valley, probably over a low pass now buried beneath the imposing volcanic edifice of Mammoth

Mountain. Air-borne ash from the eruption has been positively identified at many localities far to the east, the farthest being in Nebraska. Its volume is estimated at 150 cubic miles—about 200 times the amount erupted at Mount St. Helens on May 18, 1980.

An example of a smaller, younger, but much better known caldera is the truncated remnant of Mount Mazama known as Crater Lake, in Oregon. Presently dormant, it explosively self-destructed a little less than 7,000 years ago, disgorging as much as 12 cubic miles of pumice and ash and sending ash at least as far away as Saskatchewan, Canada. Its evolution was generally similar to that reconstructed for Long Valley, except that at Crater Lake, the development of a huge volcanic cone preceded the final paroxysmal explosion. Ragged ramparts enclosing a beautiful 6-mile-wide lake and a small interior dome, known as Wizard Island, are the most notable features remaining of the formerly vigorous volcano.

Tomorrow's Volcanoes?

Long Valley caldera has remained an intermittently active volcanic center since its violent birth nearly three-quarters of a million years ago. That Vulcan's fires are still tended, witness the thermal springs of Whitmore, Casa Diablo, and Hot Creek, and the fumaroles high on Mammoth Mountain. Long Valley has the potential to produce geothermal energy; several exploratory holes have been drilled. In fact, the best information presently available suggests that about 450 years ago residual magma from an earlier eruption rose close enough to the surface to vaporize ground water, causing the explosions responsible for the craters at the two Inyo Crater Lakes and the small craters on the north side of Mammoth Mountain. Moreover, geophysicists report evidence that suggests magma presently exists beneath Mono Craters, forming a subterranean pool about 12 miles in diameter, six or more miles beneath the surface. Volcanologists see in this enough similarity to the early stages in the development of the Long Valley caldera, to convince them that the Mono Craters area may now be in an early stage of developing into a new volcanic caldera. No one is

55

Yesterday's Volcanoes

Known in Paiute legend as "the burnt land," Long Valley and the Mono Basin have been a center of intense and often explosive volcanic activity for at least three million years. Marks of that violence are everywhere—craters, black, glassy obsidian domes, red cinder cones, light gray or reddish stony domes, acres of pumice and 450 square miles of Bishop Tuff.

Wilson Butte, erupted about 500 B.C.

Robert C. Frampton

Southern Inyo Crater, exploded about 1400 A. D.

Edwin C. Rockwell

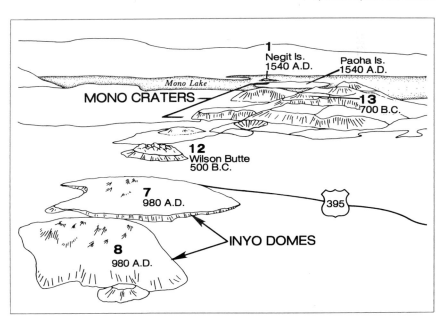

Aerial view northward of Mono Craters and two Inyo Domes. Some localities of dated eruptions and their ages shown on sketch. Localities also shown on map, p. 53.

Boiling spring, Hot Creek

La Moine R. Fantozzi

Today's Hot Springs

During this century, no one has witnessed an eruption of any kind. However, boiling springs and steam vents abound. Particularly at Hot Creek, new pools of scalding water and geysers as high as thirty feet appear and disappear unpredictably.

Tomorrow's Volcanoes?

Today's hot springs may signify the dying stages of a very long history of volcanic eruptions. More likely, they signify but a lull, a quiet chapter, in a volcanic story that is far from finished. Several geologists believe that Mono Craters and the associated ring fractures may represent early stages of caldera formation. Note the Craters' crescent shape and, on the map on page 53, how this crescent completes the circle whose west half is the Mono ring fracture. Are these features the precursors of a future "world-class" volcanic event, of Long Valley caldera proportions?

Mono Craters, Sierra Nevada in distance, Mono Lake lower left   Roland von Huene

willing to forecast the details of Mono Craters' future evolution, but there is no reluctance at all to predict at the very least a general continuation of volcanism similar to that in the recent past. This suggests that we are presently enjoying only a temporary respite from more or less continuous volcanic activity.

Recommended Reading

California Geology. Monthly publication of the California Division of Mines & Geology, P. O. Box 2980, Sacramento CA 95812. The following issues are particularly pertinent. Articles also supply valuable reference lists. Back issues available. September 1965, "The Inyo Crater Lakes—A Blast in the Past." August 1971, "Volcanism in California." March 1972, "The Great Owens Valley Earthquake of 1872." July 1979, "Seismicity of California January 1975 through March 1979." September 1980, "Mammoth Lakes Earthquakes May 25–27, 1980." August 1981, "Volcanic History and 'Active' Volcanism in California."

Iacopi, Robert. 1971. *Earthquake Country.* Lane Books, Menlo Park. Clear explanation of why California has earthquakes, followed by detailed discussion of the great San Andreas Fault that slices through western California. Also examines other major active faults, including the Owens Valley Fault. Exceptional photographs and diagrams and many of them. Admirable book, highly recommended.

Smith, Genny, Ed. 1976. *Mammoth Lakes Sierra.* Distrib. by Wm. Kaufmann, Inc., Los Altos. A trail guide for the knapsack, a road guide for the car, a field guide to the geology, plants, animals and historic points of interest.

_____. 1978. *Deepest Valley: Guide to Owens Valley.* Distrib. by Wm. Kaufmann, Inc., Los Altos. Companion book to the above.

RECOMMENDED READING

Technical Reports, all excellent sources for additional references

Bailey, Roy A., G. Brent Dalrymple and Marvin A. Lanphere. 1976. "Volcanism, structure, and geochronology of the Long Valley caldera, Mono County, California" in *Journal Geophy. Res.* v. 81, no. 5, p. 725–744.

Sherburne, Roger W. Ed. 1981. *Mammoth Lakes, California, Earthquakes of May 1980.* Special Report 150. California Division of Mines & Geology, P. O. Box 2980, Sacramento, CA 95812. A collection of papers on many aspects of the Mammoth earthquakes. Some highly technical, some not. Many excellent maps, diagrams, photographs.

Wood, S. H. 1977. "Distribution, correlation, and radiocarbon dating of late Holocene tephra, Mono and Inyo Craters, eastern California" in *Geological Society of America Bulletin,* vol 88, p. 89–95.

Two classic geologic reports

Knopf, Adolph. 1918. *A Geological Reconnaissance of the Inyo Range and the Eastern Slope of the Southern Sierra Nevada, California.* Prof. Paper 110. U.S. Geological Survey.

Russell, Israel C. 1889. *Quaternary History of Mono Valley, California.* U.S. Geological Survey, Eighth Annual Report.

62

If you've enjoyed this book and want to know more about California's magnificent Eastern Sierra, Genny Smith Books offers these other publications.

Mammoth Lakes Sierra

Fourth edition, 1976. Genny Smith, ed. By Dean Rinehart, Elden Vestal, Bettie Willard. A trail guide for the knapsack, a road guide for the car, a field guide to the geology, trees, wildflowers, mammals, fish, birds, history and all points of interest. Authoritative guide to the superbly beautiful fifty-mile portion of the eastern Sierra slope north of Owens Valley. Many maps and illustrations, 68 photographs, 192 pages, paper only.

Deepest Valley: Guide to Owens Valley, Its Roadsides and Mountain Trails

Revised edition, 1978. Genny Smith, ed. By Paul Bateman, Dorothy Cragen, Mary DeDecker, Raymond Hock, E. P. Pister. Companion book to *Mammoth Lakes Sierra*. Out of print. Revised edition due 1983.

Owens Valley Groundwater Conflict

1978. By Paul H. Lane and Antonio Rossman. Critical issues of the Inyo County lawsuit to limit groundwater pumping for the Los Angeles Aqueduct. Implications for water use throughout the West. A reprint of the new chapters in the 1978 edition of *Deepest Valley*. Maps, 28 pages, paper.

For prices and mail order information contact:

William Kaufmann, Inc.
95 First Street, Los Altos, California 94022